Around Corners
A Kid's Guide To Malaga, Spain

Photography By John D. Weigand
Poetry By Penelope Dyan

Bellissima Publishing, LLC
Jamul, California
www.bellissimapublishing.com

copyright © 2012 by Penny D. Weigand

All rights reserved. No part of this book may be
reproduced or transmitted in any form or by any means,
electronic or mechanical, including photocopying,
recording, or by any other means, or by any information or
storage retrieval system, without permission from the publisher.

ISBN 978-1-61477-032-9
First Edition

*"The world today doesn't make sense.
So why should I paint pictures that do?"*

Pablo Picasso 1881-1973

Around Corners

Bellissima Publishing, LLC

Introduction

Around every corner there is something to see wherever you go in this world. And around every corner is another corner. Award winning author, attorney and former teacher, Penelope Dyan and John D. Weigand, photographer extraordinaire, have written another travel book with a big purpose. Dyan knows what kids like to see, but sometimes they need a little help when it comes to seeing all the art surrounding them. And in this case we are exploring corners and around corners; and we are encouraging kids to explore around corners as well, and especially the corners of their minds. Malaga, Spain is the birthplace of Pablo Picasso; and it is fitting that his birthplace should inspire you to learn, paint, write and draw, especially if you explore all around all its corners. If that doesn't make any sense to you, then you are probably too old for this book. Pablo Picasso once said, "There are painters who transform the sun to a yellow spot, but there are others who with the help of their art and their intelligence, transform a yellow spot into sun." We are not here to paint a yellow spot, and no child should paint a yellow spot. A child can paint the sun! When children travel they see with the eyes of a child. It is all about signs, things alike and things different, about animals in the clouds, and dandelions they can blow and watch as seeds float in the wind; and this should be encouraged, not discouraged.

Around Corners
Bellissima Publishing, LLC

Around Corners
A Kid's Guide To Malaga, Spain

Photography By John D. Weigand
Poetry By Penelope Dyan

Pablo Picasso said, "Art is the ability
to recapture the state of childhood,"
so if you are a child that is great,
because as for being an artist,
you are not too late.
Picasso traveled all over Europe
from one corner to another,
(I would bet he always
had the support of his mother.)
He didn't travel on the duck-billed train.
Things change and are never the same.
This train is itself a work of art.
The man who designed it was very smart.

There are corners in Malaga everywhere.
Some are round and some are square.
Even a corner can be a work of art.
(You'll notice this if you are smart).
No two places are ever the same,
whether you go around a corner,
or travel by train.
Pablo Picasso was born in Malaga
October 25, 1881,
and I will bet he thought traveling
was a whole lot of fun.

Here's another corner I happened to find,
and it is of a different kind.
This corner goes in instead of out!
And corners set in corners
is what this building is all about.
You see windows round.
You see windows square.
All you have to do is to look up there!*

*Malaga´s cathedral was built between 1528 and 1782 on or near the site of a former mosque. Original plans called for two towers, lack of funds resulted in completion of only one. The cathedral is now called, La Manquita, or "one armed woman" and is next to Sagrario Church.

Around the corner I find yellow and red,
and my brain is swirling inside my head.
I think I feel a little sick;
but my mom's not worried, not one bit.

I see a corner with some trees,
and then I feel a gentle breeze.
Mom asks me if I want my sweater.
And I tell her I am feeling better.
There is just so much inside my head!
Mom says, "It's jet lag.
At home it's time for bed."

We hop aboard a double decker bus.
The top is nearly empty, except for us.
I see corners round and corners square.
And I wonder, "What's ahead up there?"
Around every corner is a new surprise,
a feast for any artist's little eyes.

I see some buildings that are navy blue
and bright, bright yellow,
Mom says the architect was quite clever
and very, very wise.
They look something like
the condominiums at home,
but they're *all* wearing a disguise!

And then I hear the church bells ring.
If we go inside will the choir sing?*

*Museo y Basílica de Santa María de la Victoria

We go to the top of the hill and look down.
Below us is practically the entire town!
I take a deep breath full of fresh air.
There are loads of corners right down there.
Mom says it is a feast for the eyes,
behind every corner, I'll find a surprise!
Colors, shapes and shadows fill this space.
A smile grows upon my face.

This building looks like fun.
We've seen a lot, but we're not done.*

*Ayuntamiento (City Hall)

What oh what do I see?
I see two green parrots in a tree.
I watch but do not linger long.
I don't want to interrupt the parrots' song.
I always watch silently in my explore,
Around the corner I know there's more.*

* *"Everyone wants to understand painting. Why is there no attempt to understand the song of the birds?"*

PABLO PICASSO

Even the lighthouse* (although round)
has corners, I see,
at its base next to the trees.
For me Malaga has been a lot of fun!
But now it is time to paint the sun!*

*Málaga City Lighthouse, "La Farola" 1817

* "There are painters who transform the sun to a yellow spot, but there are others who with the help of their art and their intelligence, transform a yellow spot into sun." Pablo Picasso

"The chief enemy of creativity is good sense."

PABLO PICASSO

www.ingramcontent.com/pod-product-compliance
Lightning Source LLC
LaVergne TN
LVHW071652060526
838200LV00029B/434